CANANDAIGUA

ALICE JAMES BOOKS
New Gloucester, ME
alicejamesbooks.org

CANAN

DONALD REVELL

DAIGUA

10 9 8 7 6 5 4 3 2 1

Alice James Books are published by Alice James Poetry Cooperative, Inc.

Alice James Books
Auburn Hall
60 Pineland Drive, Suite 206
New Gloucester, ME 04260
www.alicejamesbooks.org

Library of Congress Cataloging-in-Publication Data

Names: Revell, Donald, 1954– author.
Title: Canandaigua / Donald Revell.
Description: New Gloucester, ME : Alice James Books, 2024.
Identifiers: LCCN 2023053356 (print) | LCCN 2023053357 (ebook)
   ISBN 9781949944624 (trade paperback) | ISBN 9781949944341 (epub)
Subjects: LCGFT: Poetry.
Classification: LCC PS3568.E793 C36 2024 (print) | LCC PS3568.E793
   (ebook) | DDC 811/.54--dc23/eng/20231116
LC record available at https://lccn.loc.gov/2023053356
LC ebook record available at https://lccn.loc.gov/2023053357

Alice James Books gratefully acknowledges support from individual
donors, private foundations, and the National Endowment for the Arts.

ART WORKS.
arts.gov

Cover image: George Hitchcock. *The Annunciation*, 1887. The Art Institute
of Chicago.

IN MEMORY OF RICHARD L. HARP,
TRUE FRIEND AND SCHOLAR

CONTENTS

I

They cannot fool us with how fast they go,
How much they cost each other and the gods.

—W.H. AUDEN,
"Woods"

OUTRAGE

A new tree uprooted and thrown
Into the street fire knows
The brief agony of the Absolute,
A Dantescan moment, and then
The deformity of fire.
Justice is a poor sort without
A living tree. Comfort the angry boys
Out of your green air, as once
A stranger tree overpowered hellfire.
Love is absolute, and justice
Shelters like an insect at its root.
Inevitable morning, inevitable ash
Covers agony with soft light
And slow light, on our familiar streets.

LIGHT, ZEAL

Like echoes incarnate, sparrows trouble
A scorched willow with sound and flutter.
Old Adam catches a whisper
Out of Eden, aching but warm to it.
The imagination does harm, real harm.
As Pascal says, it is a bold indolence,
Magnifying almost nothing until
Branches break beneath the empty weight.

In the first days of the pandemic,
A peahen came to live in our yard.
Weeks later, at first light, I found,
In its full display, a white peacock
Facing her. The smaller birds fell silent,
Gathered into crowns on the black tree,
Silent. Boldness and nothingness in pride
Imaged the soul of fire whispering

Out of Eden future Edens, a dozen
Names for every creature, and new green
Buds on the dead willow. Impossible
To find any harm in extravagance taking
Refuge, undertaking the old purposes of
Creation. But harm there was. There was

Interruption, zeal without knowledge, awe
Where tenderness ought to have looked away.

Pascal writes: "Where is God? Where you are not,
And the kingdom of God is within you."
In extravagance, all measure is desire,
Scorched earth, and menacing vapor —
Tatterdemalion adoring itself.
Inherit the earth. Invent the earth.
In pride and display, harm is done. Adam
Hears the bitter echo of his beginning.

A DEFENSE OF POETRY

The long era of mothering atoms and slow clocks,
Seven centuries at least since the Gothic
Signature—*Adamo me fecit*—made stones come alive,
Alerting the level ground to distances
Of wildflowers and white rabbits that knew Christ, knew him
In his captivity as the brown man bled
White, lying among them, a kind of lacework, ends now.

We are adrift in oblivion's azure.
The oldest among us remember clouds
Bellied like golden sheep in the afternoons,
Slowly pasturing into nights that meant no harm.
The young remember only grievance against
Clouds, and no wonder. To them, the sky has always been
A barrier to peaceful protest, and protest

Is the only earthly purpose they have known.
In New York, the unicorn tapestries turn
Their faces to the wall. The white rabbits abandon
The embroidered borders of Incarnation.
How many wildflowers can I name before the names
Die out of my English? There remain some few
Gothic bones unaccounted for in human bodies,

Nameless, but bearing a signature. And clouds,
Piling upon themselves in towers, are also words
Addressed to barriers: the babble God loves.

Wildflowers of this world grow as high as Heaven's gate.
Shall we, for *Chrissakes* stop this foolishness and
Begin to read what we ourselves have written, measure
The anthems of humanity by human strides?

SPARTOI

They are nothing if not modern,
And they are not modern. Parented
At length and learnedly, they
Revel in ancestry even as they
Brightly surpass the cringe
And calumny of ancestors.
Modernity, descended since Adam
From childlessness, identifies
Only with pain of death and
Phoenix fires. Entirely elsewhere,
It shepherds some few into shadows.
Beauty follows, knowing, by instinct,
The harms, arising like teeth
Out of the ground, which Progress,
In absolute enmity, intends it.
Often disappointed but never
Surprised, the Modern ruins
A soldiery out of the sky,
Fearless of posterity yet careful
Of any embroidered animal,
Hare or songbird, taking fright.

COMMUNARDS

in memory of my cousin, Diane Smith

1.

Just now, it was the malice of a cup,
This brown cup. What did Haussmann give
To Paris or Robert Moses to New York? A cup,
Very much like this one, and the malice of it,
Emptiness ready to hand and ready
To forbid a boy his beloved cousin
In traffic, the idiocy of human greed.

We feel the change, shun
The little things, and hurry —
That ivy, this wren,
Rain as it may —

Because strangeness is speed.
I am with them.
As sun suffers shade,
I am with them.

This isn't going away, this
Mean-spirited, progressive tumult:
Kettle to cup, pale cousin to interstate
Commerce carting a flag as though
It were a babe in arms. No babies

For my cousin. No aftermath to the hand
In hand of kinship, kinship simple, kinship slow.
Our common prayer had nowhere to go.

2.

Ne cede malis, and in the language
Of those one cannot hope to emulate.
Virgil coined a perfect motto for The Bronx,
And Robert Moses put it to the test. We couldn't
Walk a step in any direction. The gates
Of the underworld were opened wide
Always, and yet we couldn't walk. My fatal
Cousin and I were rhyming communards.

To feel the change, choose
A book and tear its pages
Into the wind. Loose
Words, brief altitudes,

These are the progress
Made in the name of
Progress, oh seasons,
Oh châteaux of vowels.

Ivy grows backwards into the wren's hot nest.
Rain slows to a whisper of white metal.
Suffering shade, the sun dives underground,
Buckling the interstates. Did you know
A city can thrive in complete ignorance
Of other cities? Plantations of thin air

Feed millions. I am eating my words.
My cousin and I were rhyming communards.

3.

Disney and the Metaphysicals, men
Equally impossible to emulate
As our theaters fill with emptiness,
As our poems go lame into the lean dearth
Of their English. Progress, the antithesis
Of change, is surely the Muse of Malice.
Slow change, antique nursery of music,
Joy, and eternity, happens in little
Streets among the cartoon animals
And fire escapes. Progress, on the other hand,
Is exactly what John Berryman
Imagined it to be: a cancer with a plan.
New York's ruined anatomy, Rimbaud's
Gang rape are only comprehensible
As whispering, hastening, white-hot metal.
My cousin's barrenness in the full flush
Of her beauty only accounts to God
As God, in His own beauty, changes all.
I am a fit of rhyme against rhyme,
A commune of no one but the wren.
Wretched Diane and I were beasts in all
But integrity, not won but freely given.
Must one think of everything as earned?
Do birds divorce? Across the street, no
Distance at all, a naked thinking heart
Walks into traffic. There was nowhere else to go.

4.

Does laughter brutalize? Ask the rebar
In a busted wall or, better still, ask
Buster Keaton. He, better than any,
Knew the malice of inanimate things
Inspired suddenly with strangeness:
Avalanche without a mountain; traffic
Deaths on a blank screen or an empty street.
He knew that Progress is a maniac.

I feel the changeable moon
Divorcing Earth.
It has no face to show us
Just now, only a pallor of vowels,

Swan's down soiled with earth.
There are velocities
Like cities swallowing air
Out of thin air and dying of it.

This isn't going away. Cup in hand,
A forbidden boy goes begging across
The exit ramps. Worlds away, his cousin,
Clothed in ivy and feathers, carries
Her child into a ruined château.
The evening air is underscored with magic.
God is calling the moonlight back to heaven.

GUESSING GAME

If this is a skill set, heaven help you.
Left to right, three cages appear to be
Embedded in three mountains of increasing
Grandeur. In each cage, there is a small boy,
Naked, struggling with a heavy chain.
I have chosen a name for each of the mountains.
Guess the names, and the little boys go free.

I am near death because of the death of allegory.
America also, because it lacks the vocabulary.
A cathedral, with little stalls for selling things,
Settles into a great rift of apathy.
Breughel screams. Lincoln hears. A polyphony
Of antic, actually human sounds,
Disappears into the mountains. Free the boys.

IN MEMORY OF
JEAN VALENTINE

1.

A three-quarters moon is quick this New Year's morning,
Almost transparent at the tip of those mountains.
There are no bears. The kitchen window, propped open
By an old dictionary (blue Larousse), eases
Cold air and a few last flecks of starlight inside.
Last night, we played at tall puppets and perfected
A most imperfect year with your death's gaiety:
Pencils and bears. You were the life of the party.

2.

Under the night's final lamp, I found a stranger's
Writing in your books: a scatter of emphases,
A few translations and, more than once, the one word
"Emmanuel" underscored. It was all in soft
Pencil, easy to erase if I wanted to.
I didn't. In the red hymnal given to me
In 1961 "for good conduct," the word
"Emmanuel" is likewise underscored, page two,
The second hymn for Advent. Clearly, the stranger
Knew us. Knew us in just the way tips of mountains
Know the disappearing moon. The kitchen window
Stays open to emphasis. I believe in ghosts.

3.

For the most part, the advantage of a New Year
Fades as the sun erases the image of indoors
From all the windows, leaving only the old worlds
Of transparency and printed pages in books
Left open upon disappearing night tables.
The same anew, as every tippler knows who once
Has leaned against the sun. Time heals nothing until
Time is no more. I remember the two of us
Running late—me for the airport, you for the bus
Station after a high old time at Wesleyan.
We made our connections, clumsily, but made them.
Safe at home, we saw the Great Bear at our windows.

STAND

in memory of Robert D. Richardson

The solid ground is prose, and the prose
Of death is stubborn and rock-hard
With this question: Can I stand
The universe? In the great earthquake,
William James ran outdoors, shouting
"Go it! Go it!" So I can stand it,
Alright, and in John 16 Christ says
"I have overcome the world."
These efforts are beyond America,
But essential. The tightening
Of our heartstrings as we say "Yes"
(Meaning "I'm afraid") fixes
The republic to a shadow and to a fictional
Sunrise. I had a friend once, long
Before sunrise, and his shadow
Only lengthens in death, effortlessly
As new days did in the old days.
What an expression: *The old days*!
I've never seen one. Poetry
Is the groundless belief in fearful
Attention. Heartstrings bind
Horizons onto the real sun.
We might live forever. Go it.

THE ARCHAIC

Arid, desolate, and nearest me,
Those mountains wester meanings
Out of existence, where the meanings
Stay. Anything farther is fires.
Like you, I have a forest to mourn,
Corresponding to God, as God
Walked through the woods and the woods
Vanished behind Him. Faith
Is the archaic praise of that vanishing.
We are ghosts who believe, and beneath
The dirt over there is a golden wall
Dividing all the beauty of this world
Into twinned fires and snowcapped
Desolations. I very nearly saw
A bighorn o'erleap the flames,
Archaic sentinel without a trace
Westering to where his vigil ends.

IN MEMORY OF
YVES BONNEFOY

Enjoying the shelter of a single tree
With the rain just ending, with the grass
Already standing upright and curious,
Annihilation and immortality
Shared words before going their separate ways.

The first of these was "footsteps." Someone walking
Behind Cædmon whispered to him about wings
And setting foot upon ladders. Poetry
Was inevitable, as were animals
To croon, to wonder, to stride on calm waters

And change. Curiosity about angels
Is surely the broad syllable of all life
Amazed by a certain climbing up and down
In bones, in feathers and eyesight. First footsteps,
And then the sudden changes further our flight.

LARRY DIES

Men are gabbing in three languages
Not one of them understands.

Clematis is a fourth.

And so the sun is stilled in its still agenda,
Rusted beneath the broken swings
On soft earth.
So many had come so far to play
Who cannot play, who cannot,
In this broken economy, find the shade to say
Clematis.

Flowers wear the bright detention colors.
Some dogs bark. The flowers darken.

Let us be friends and not die,
Or let us mow and die.

A MUSTARD TREE

Is an extravagance, a parable
Of nonexistence without nests,
And no more trouble than confetti.

A bird's weight might bend it to earth.
How then should it rise again? Again,
Perhaps wings and a skeletal weight

Edged with death and sunlight
Have heaven to answer and heave
Upwards. Can you believe it?

I would love to see one thing in this world
Tireless. I imagine wings
All by themselves, without bodies,

Filling the whole sky. Homeless
Save for direction, and that always
Upwards, they are daylight's darlings,

A species of prism that neither fails
Nor falls. Think of rain, if rain
Were a separate mirror of the sun.

Nonexistence is not an obstacle.
The least and the greatest lodge together
In extravagance. There was never

Any need for the nebulae to be
So beautiful, nothing sheltering there,
No birds to believe or weight to bear.

Gratuitous beauty proves the leaven
Of cosmos and of the last moment
Before waking, our foothold in Heaven.

A lissome grass grows into empty space.
It grows wings, and earth pays it small attentions:
Shadows here and there; weddings in Cana.

L'ESILIATO RIENTRAVA NEL PAESE INCORROTTO

It never occurred to me—
The scent of the past,
As of a broken stem of rosemary
In my hand just now,
With the sun whitening the ground
And no air, none at all, so that
Scent travels like a knife wound
Bled out of memory,
It never occurred to me—
The scent of the past really
Penetrated the young as they were
Truly young in bone and mind
Which are mine now, soothing
Their white deaths a little and
Youthfulness also, blooded
With the scent of rosemary.

SHEPHERD OF ALL SORTS

To love as if always at the edge of sleep,
A south wind of words at the eaves, colors
Each of which inclines gently, cactus beneath
Snowdrift in decades, in perfected sequence
From the year Zero, and then Zero again,
Jubilates the poem beyond all caution.

The next step, to separate love from knowledge,
Teases the dream into winter light, Janus
At the horizon moving both ways
Where an infant sun is twinned, and one
Twin dies. There is no intimacy
In caution, in waking. Truth is a cold house.

Unless. Walking the incline slowly, peering
Into one house after another, finding
A different calendar in each, and every
Calendar the broken door of a decade,
You take a moment to love and to perish
Upon the woodwork and the windblown snow inside.

Knowing ends with death. Love walks on. A wholly
New version of sleep, a life of lowering
Clouds on rooftops, hilltops, shepherds of all sorts
Stepping out of shadows into newborn
Light, begins to quicken nil with integers,
As language quickens with simple animals.

Unless Adam. At the edge of sleep, which was
Adam's very beginning, a garden of
Colors and anonymity, creatures
Simply walked into their names as if walking
Out of a storm and into shelter, into
Warm calendars concealing a bitter truth.

Truth is a cold house. History is backwards
Unless what is human in us dreams across
Our own humanity without caution, with
Only zero and jubilation in mind.
Knowledge dies at the foot of its bad tree.
An infant sun is twinned, and both survive.

ASKED AND ANSWERED

While Europe vanishes, our day becomes
Itself. First among birdsong and the last,
The sound of it covers roots, covers
Branches and all of the horizon. Who are
These strangers bent upon vanishing? Asked
And answered, as in the allegory
I fear you have forgotten, the perfect one
In which a songbird escapes beyond hearing
Into Heaven. Transcendence isn't something
To toy with. If the trees are disappearing,
Surely this day, of all days, must see
The horizon stand up into the sky
In terror and walk, both sunrise and sunset
Nested in the levels of its stride.

THE IRRETRIEVABLE

Second shelf on the right. You'll
   Never find it. Given
      Our father's cold centennial—

When the snow was too big to fall
   But hovered in midair as though the air
      Had opened white lips

Meaning to speak to us, to say
   Something about immortality and correction—
      We ought to abandon the search.

Or should I say "the seeking"?
   Shelving the town, four cliffs
      Evangelize these misgivings.

Second on the right is what became
   Of a drunkard obsessed with
      Chapter 14 in the Gospel of John.

It's a gospel secretly given
   To hawks, not to eagles.
      Topography emboldens love when hawks

Shatter their prey midair out of pure spite.
   Mansions of devastation scatter themselves
      Into big snow. Our father's

Cold centennial had a further child,
  Hidden from us. In the days ahead she
    Will ease us — little predator, little ice.

THE CATTLE

Not even a moment,
A narrow gap in the pillars
Of...Heaven? sheer exhaustion?...
Widened, disclosing a halo
Of few words, thus
My Nebraska. Thus a green distance
Briefly gilded the darkness underneath.

I was more tired than I knew.
In less than a moment, the few
Words ample to all poems bent
Horizon into a Mercator crown.
Beloved syllables echoed the shapes
Of cattle. Flecks of real gold
Shone in their eyes on me.

MY VOCABULARY

Angel of my loves, I cannot
Anymore capture the smallest words,
Your wings as once you
Closed them upon me and the night ended.
Nothing moves freely in me.
The sun's a legend with no biography.
Bedsheets disappear into the garden noise,
Making shadows. If I were to ask the roses,
Only one would know your name.

Nothing moves without invisible consent.
And I'm not thinking of powers, but rather
Of smiles hidden, of the semen and metal
In window glass when the glare of sudden rain
Blinds it. Permit the angel, and your permission
Lifts Dante out of a dead faint. Permit
The free exchange of small words
In sleep and, as the sun rises, wings
Close upon the words, then a rose, then nothing.

CREON'S DREAM

The birds are Sophoclean,
  Paired peahens
    Nested side by side to no
Purpose.

And as the heat of summer
  Becomes a hammer
    Taken to the rain
Mercilessly,

The Sophoclean birds
  Roll in the dirt,
    Covering themselves as
Antigone

Ought to have done and did
  In her hot, hanged
    Dream in the cave of God's
Mercy.

There is never enough grief.
  When the birds scream
    Into the dirt where is no
Shelter,

No relief, haphazard trees
  Blind the eyes
    In their beautiful feathers.
Something

In the beauty of things defies
  Tragedy and pities
    The dirt and the noise of hammers across
Rain.

II.

So what is faith if it is not
inescapable endurance?

— GEOFFREY HILL

WHITSUN 2020

Heat like a hammer blow to the eye,
Soundless and without atmosphere,
Circles the willow, and the wasps fall
Dead in it. There is no fire. Of the four
Elements, none takes the imprint of
Humanness now and here. From the Latin
Salire, to leap, the willow, *Salix*,
Has nowhere to go. Virgil is long gone
From our fuss. There was a carcass,
Lord god of the bees, but it was
Carted away. Heat is human
Personality without persons.
The cold heaven knows it. Saints there
Busy themselves with strange honey.
They also grow the French *noir de Verlaine*
And the orange-stemmed golden willow.

EXILIC

Sunlight stills the wind, the wilder
Swan, one moment before a moment of color,
As lavender calms lions. Fast and loose,
Fast and loose with the truth, these altars
Of our English do actually on the line
Strip, sacrifice, and so tenderly crown
Treetop with treetop, grass blade with the swan's
Whiteness, like a chrism of whiteness: sunlight.

I see that Giotto invented mountains,
The first mountains, just as Christ planted
Eyes in Giotto's head for treetops. Loveliness
Is landscape's intellection: lavender
Comes to mind. Come tenderly and see
The mountain range on a grass blade's whited
Edge. Altarwise, as someone said, meaning
Stone of sacrifice, all for the sake of trees.

The very image of a blind man's dream
Fixes the earth upon its axis. Color
Conceals itself below the horizon, then
Bursts into being: a mountain for Giotto;
A solitary boat in trailing willow
Branches for one man in Asia; and for the saints,
A whirling intelligence in their bones,
Meaning a breeze freshened out of Heaven.

And yet Jerome was not Jerome, nor was there ever
A wilderness. I see now, treetops and mountains
Gather grammars into a kind of skating,
And the saints glide right out of existence.
Their intellections were lions in the lavender.
We ought to empty the museums sometimes.
As New York is lined up for hours for Jerome,
We ought to let the miraculous preaching end

Where it began: the fabulous partition
In a painted heart. Look inwards, farther in
And deeper than the heart's little hermitage.
Mister, there is your soul, a cognate
Of gleaming distances beyond all grammars.
Magdalene and Lazarus disembark
At Marseilles, where there are larks for sale.
Would it kill you, Mister, to buy one?

The caged lark and the wilder swan, neither
Contravenes the chrism of whiteness I
Imagined in a dark place—that part of myself
Below the heart cut by Christ with a grass blade
Into mountains, mountains, and a forest of English.
It's funny to find oneself in a tradition
Up a tree. The blinded man climbs down, takes root.
He's been dreaming, and his soul has a willow wand.

Below the heart, there is a moment of flesh
In which the soul imagines itself without words,
Without images. Mister, think of a simple
Melody you've forgotten but truly loved.

Perhaps a girl climbs into a tree. Maybe
A river spills one of its secrets, and a city,
The city of your birth, appears out of nowhere.
Fast and loose is how the Lord made us.

HIDE AND SEEK

Why remember? I answer
With roses, those dark houses
Of radiant doorways. Home
Before dark was the first
Injunction of childhood,
An answered prayer before
Anyone had prayed it,
As one blood-red rose
Repeated itself over and over
On the bedroom wallpaper.
Believe the wallpaper, all-
Ye-outs-in-free.

Memory is best alone, tilting
A little nearer the light of one
Lamp. One hand finds another,
The duplicate of itself, praying.
For a moment, someone standing
Just outside the circle of lamplight,
Yourself for instance, might
See a blood-red rose cupped
Between two hands. Turn away.
Other worlds and their low, radiant
Doorways are jealous beyond words.
Go straight home.

WHITE-JACKET

Alive snow, and motive
Like swans in grief, in anger
Powers the sky, and one life
Is the bitter aftertaste of that snow
Lingering. Have you chosen,
At last, a century or even
One soft corner of the waterfront?

See the nautical men in midair.
See the fabulous author
Kneeling at the end of his cold pier.

The times are timid and overturned.
The snow falls short of the receiving
Ocean. Bellying canvas lures
Wild swans to destruction.
Was it ridicule or rancor
That brought the author to his knees?
There is strange cargo in the written word,
And ideal animals, and no harbor.
For all the good it does, the snow is alive.

DYING

Something overlong, lungs and brainpan,
And no woman there. Tithon would remark
Emptiness where once there shone
A benison, a long and small. Imagine
Anthems in repose, although the music
Stammers a bit upon waking, as the sun
Curves to accommodate mountains. I breathe.
I think of faces, each lifted and withheld,
With history and its Homeric swineherds
Crowded against a kiss. Birds feed on faces.
Eyes whiten with the frenzy of them, nearly
Sightless but with the prick of daylight showing
A passage to the afterlife, not overlong
But narrow, and the ground shifting beneath me.

FOR JOHN RUSKIN

St. Ursula dreams a distant
   Sprig of vervain.
      It comes to her bedside, arriving

Green and quickly via
   Supple angels:
      Precisely those angels

You will not permit, even *in extremis*, me.

Ursula, still in the dream,
   Whispers in her chapel voice,
      "Thorn" and "bramble"

Onto the vervain as though
   A low plant sacred to travelers
      Might actually restrain

One supple angel. Permit me

Even that one, and I'll go quietly
   To the date far distant,
      A wand of nothing in my fist.

The traffic of a girl in actual sainthood
  Whispers under wood
    All night, whispers fire

Across a road in me, lost until now.

PROGRESSIONS

Someone, not a god,
Has dropped a book
Onto the concert floor.
The sound alters the music.

Sound before and sound afterward, with every book merely
An interval, a distraction from hot originals:
Say "Aleph" or say the whisper of an old flame beneath
A bed of ashes. The book burned before it was written.

While in 1932, Helen Hayes
In *A Farewell to Arms* correctly
Pronounces the name MAR-vell
(Not mar-VELL) in a true love scene—

Noises ravished by syllables. I have seen it happen
On a woman's mouth or, now, in a civilization
Turning against a few words, all of them mewed expressions
Of love, aborted vocables. Have we had world enough and time?

A name dropped not
By a god, nor by anyone

Living now, living now.
The music was altered.

It continues. Savagery growls into the manias.
Wooden bellies of string instruments bloat and echo nonsense.
I like to believe any number of books, hovering
Like fires inside fires, might never touch the ground.

A dull sound, a thud
In 2021 rests upon
The concert floor, godless
Music distracted but continuing.

DISTANT SIRENS

Of youth transfigured in the deer,
A pair newly mated, and the awful
Hours between X and Y, all
In a clearing, a white elliptical
Stand of birches surrounding,
Observe the harm already done
And the risk of harms greater still.

A coruscation of heat lightning
Sets fire to the trees. Youth
Is wasted. Distant sirens
Frighten sparrows into the deer path.
Youth is helpless unless, transfigured
Between X and Y, it imagines
A new animal and becomes

The twin of itself with malice.
Imagination is the greater harm.
The young buck covers the doe
And the whole clearing rises,
Shrieking sparrows and all, out
Of the birches, into a black lake
Of sky. Smoke is not air.

LARGO

Schubert was poorly. Sun motes danced an arc
Of emptiness over the lens of Vienna, and staves,
Rivers of them, purled towards the brute frontier.
Romance is the kindergarten of savagery.
Striving for health, music presses backwards
Against time, against the walking woods
And bleached-out sunlight of tomorrow — tomorrow
Morning worst of all. A clear lens, a stave
Crowded with sharps and signatures, opens
Onto a hastening multitude in old clothes — they
Were the music, once upon a time, returning
Ragged and boisterous from Arcady.
Schubert is among them, youthful and macabre.
The sun is the Romani walking beside him.

HERESY

A glisten of wind inside the palms, intermittent
Predators—the hawk, the dragonfly also
Shining there—signal to the ground. This is
The new portrait. Not a Parisian or a boy
With his back turned to the viewer, his back
The kind of velvet with which all youth
Mocks mortality. Rather, the figure
In question questions eyesight even as it stoops,
Bites down into the meat of the viewer and his
Nonsense. What are we seeing? Portraiture
Has simply walked out of the world with God.
The ground beneath us is bloodshed and mayhem.
Hawk bites air. Dragonfly feasts upon the film
Of waters. Youth has no world but to choose a world
And then to consume it as quickly as possible.

Eyesight was a flower when the sun meant something.
Nothing was ugly. Voracity was the soul of virtue, I mean
The green cord *vertu* with which Chaucer bound
Predator to prey and God to the shine in treetops.
Every child was more a child than we
Imagine. Youth faced front. You could make its portrait
Sleeping on the wing, waking to find yourself
Nested in a head of hair, a hand's breadth,
Or a pair of eyes exactly the shape of your own
Except green as eyes have never been so green.
There was no room for death when the sun meant something.

The trees were full, striking down hot roots
Of hunger and replenishment into childlikeness.
One day a girl penciled a red heart into the earth.
It was an enticement—archaic and isolated.

Hawk is an image of himself hunting. The sun,
Which once had shone beneath his wings, shrinks
To a pinprick, to a bloodletting of small eyes.
This is the new portrait. Image, not courtesy,
Distinguishes lover from beloved,
Dragonfly from the flicker of dragonfly
Across water. Murder is usual
On the back of murder, that clever boy
Who will not turn to face me, choosing instead
Abyss and backwardness in the old sunlight.
The boy was myself on a better day, or you
And I together when we believed our books.
What are we seeing? Penciled into the earth,
Strange affections thwart the clay-cold worm.
Something ruthless glistens in the trees.

I think we are meat now, and we must look upon
Even beloved eyes as menace and predation.
Divided among voracious flowers, the sun,
Our Kansas of slow growth and certainty, was quickly
Devoured. No portrait survives, nor any
Seed of light. Imagery simply walked
Out of the world, taking its own sweet time
As well as all the books and the clever boys
Out of the picture. Courtesy has taken to the trees.
Something unintelligible has replaced birdsong,
Something made of consonants and anger.

The underwood shrieks at sinking humanity,
One hairpiece and one straw hat at a time. I saw a movie
Once, very much like it, when I was on velvet,
And the hand inside my pocket was not mine.

THE SEASON TO SCALE

A day too large for the summer, standing up
Out of the bus lanes, puzzled on its face
Like the miniaturist who became famous
In the corner of his garage and rose up
Out of scraps and dolls' heads into a loneliness
Too big for his heart or for his fingers' ends.
Today is like that. Today I was discharged
From hospital after a brief illness
And all the undirected passion of illness,
A poor still life aspiring to the dark edge
And depth of landscape. Today is too large,
And my heart shrinks at the center of it.

On the wards, fact and truth wear the same gowns,
Receive the same treatment at arm's length.
But outside, beyond the ziggurats and shallow
Climates of the medical city, you
Must tell them apart. You need to know
That one is the civil traffic of the hour,
The life and outwardness of the bus lanes,
And that the other is the nearly immobile
Victim of each day, and in particular,
Of the large days whose treetops and hidden
Parklands spread across the city and sky
Until you need no heart and your heart dies.

Everyone, in a moment of good health,
Finds a razor-shadow of perfect celebration
Between the flower and the leaf,
Between the sunlit facts
And truth's coronal grief
Over the huge, sure end of celebration
In the next moment. That's the fun of health,

Its joyous but cool, kind attention
To smallness, to the displaced elves of happiness
That survive as ghosts
Within the thinning shade,
As original facts
After the diaspora of attention
That is an aspiration to real happiness,

The depth of landscape. Almost everyone
Gets lucky. Health strays quickly into passion
Where it is full summer
And each hot day is larger
And much easier
Thanks to the untruthful bus services of passion.
The sheer scale of it could stop the heart in anyone.

The miniaturist returned gladly to obscurity,
A fool for size, but too crazy to change.
I take large steps away from the hospital.
I am wearing the fresh, more modest and more
Durable gown of a large day in summer
In a great city whose rapacious amenities
Do the people's thinking and prescribe
The health and heartlessness that will sustain them.

In my place in line at the bus stop
I feel a foolishness coming over me,
A passion for the big picture. The man next to me
Suddenly brightens a little in a moment

Of heat lightning and then is like myself again:
Undetailed, conventional, and aspiring
To landscapes already receding with the storm
That did not break. The plain facts of our lives
Are like that. And truth is where it rains
On a damp, immobile garden only a fool would leave.
I remember my first trip to Brooklyn.
I took a bus before dawn, and then the subway.
When I came up into the light, a bad storm
Had already come and gone through the city. Trees
Lay stripped and fallen, but the sky was clear blue.
I felt a perfect celebration like a piano's still insides.

REVELATION

I'd almost forgotten thunder,
   Lightning, and the kindly
      Showmanship of death. John

Of Patmos, as it turns out,
   Was gentler in his half-mad showings
      Than these United States or nature.

Nature came to the end of itself
   And, having spent itself, invented
      Death. Humans, inveterate showmen

Attached to God and to God's marvelous
   Resilience (e.g. the walnut, the dung beetle,
      The animal nebulae on show to astronomers),

Gathered a windfall of white petals
   And of syllables where death had come and gone.
      Early on, America imagined a stallion

Bred from the syllables, but nothing
   Came of it but broken fence lines and broken
      Flowers hung on the wire. So much death,

So little showmanship. Ends determine everything.
   A sad attachment to beginnings mistakes
      Wildness and, mistaking wildness, it ruins

Liberty: liberty upon a branch
   Hardening into food; liberty eating shit
      In slow fury; liberty setting fire to the emptiness

Between stars. Nature's say says nothing.
   Look for signature lightning in the night sky.
      It frightens animals, and it frees you.

THE PLANET

The issue
  Albeit quickly sketched
    In the manner of Giacometti
Might burn...

And then again the life of any human
  (Issue of?
    An angel
A clockwinder)

Burns with equal haste,
  Loving so much
    And loving poorly.

Are we perhaps deciding the fate of Earth?

On the far side
  Of the farthest cloud
    A pencil sketch
Of a boy destined for life everlasting

Drifts across the sun.
  For a moment his eyes
    Flare ages of insight.
Something has been decided.

Wind the clocks backwards
  Until they break, but something
    Has been decided,
White as the white harvest in Samaria.

ARRIVAL AT EMMAUS

I looked into the moon for influence and found none,
Neither ebb nor flood. Brutus was, once again,
Mistaken. Mariners and assassins move alone
Into the drift of things, and the moon's a friend
Only to sunrise and to the sharp smoke arising
From the clamor of birds whose fires are wings.

How well the Earth goes on without the benefit of
History. Hatched by May moonlight, fireflies
Keep their rumors of the sun alive until sunrise
All summer long. Such faith is perfect love
Drifting through the grass that blackens and then shines brightly
Through Philippi, wildfires, smoke and tyranny.

Meanwhile the ocean, a tyranny of its own in steely
Contention with the moon, drowns the halcyon.
We are restless. Befriended and then friendless, we look
To the tide charts, star charts, white hands full of smoke
Whose influence is drift and a pale eye for pallor.
What is the use of whiteness at the new moon?

If he is my friend, I can see right through him. Whiteness
Pales to translucence, and then an empty sky
Receives him into emptiness, into the future
I fear more even than I fear extinction:
Mountains crouched into labor; low clouds collecting alms
Out of the constant traffic; death a streetlight.

My friend has made another friend, and we three travel
A road of smoke and fallen birds whose eyes gleam
With greenfly. Insects and perfection make for easy
Going. The moon wastes away. White mountains clasp
Clouds to their dying fall. I call for madder music,
Stronger influence, a clamor to raise me.

We are three, and Emmaus welcomes our long shadows.
Ask Caravaggio, who had the good sense
Always to keep the moon indoors—the future never
Frightens one who is a horizon to himself.
Smoke rises out of broken bread. Obscure texts suddenly
Come clear. Yes, the assassins were mariners

All along. The heavens had never been an issue.
It was always smoke, and smoke becoming wings
Of birds, of fireflies, of a very few plain words
Whose beauty could not influence the outcome.
Surely, through many terrors, the oceans rise
To meet new souls adrift in clamor.

PSALTERY

The geese above her sounding more like dogs, a doe
Leaps out of the thaw into bigger trees.
Day becomes itself, hardly broken at all.
Some things love the world too well to go on
Living. Others, under the aegis of better noise
Or of snow not melted beneath the saints,
Face it out midair, leaping forever
Out of the thaw and into bigger trees.
Either way, the doe escapes. Nothing else matters.
Either the trees catch fire from the snow,
Which only God could explain, or, leaping,
She accomplishes a new constellation,
Shining cold starlight onto the trees, which only
God, in the climates of His pleasure, could allow.

THISTLE

"Thistledown is clouds," says Actual Man,
"come down to earth to cover the churches."
Light is the color of walls between life
And death. Brief shadows of eclipse
Race like foxy clouds, but the dead move slowly,
As slowly as windows in walls when light
Barely shows through. If an actual man
Is present, the color of blood appears,
Rust of the foxtail between cupboard
And narthex. New York feels a tremor of barrage.
If only a ghost or candle of ghost,
All color backwards through a prism goes
To anathema — Manhattan's actual
Glands and wounds below the wall.

Either resurrection or the tall stain
Mistaken for a mountain actually
Begins with a human face, as a city begins
On the lips of a dying man dreaming
One last dream, and you and I will spend
Eternity there. Manhattan walls itself off.
The continent abolishes its mountains.
The Chrysler Building writes a novel
About an immigrant writing a novel.
I'd meant to love a woman with wires of hair,
But I love you. Eternity has a taxi
All to itself. Rain, rain. Your hand touches

My hair, and we must keep walking. We must
Remember to pray. God was a mountain once.

Once the motive of memory, the accosted
Child, becomes real, it is free of memory.
Becoming an actual man, he plays
At a cat's cradle of fantasticals.
A faun, if you like, a perpetual
Curtain of hairs falling upon theatrical
New York. He is the eclogue of us.
Do the pronouns worry you? Do the taller
Buildings seem to menace little churches
Of cloud and eclipse in the alleyways?
A prism of blood in your own heart
Sets you straight. And prayer comes easily then.
You needn't remember your heart to beat it.
I have eaten words for sixty years, no harm done.

The crooked arm of the expressway bends
Up and away from the street life, the cloudy
Worship of numbers parallel to faith.
"Victorious victimhood!" So laments
Or so begins the Actual Man's mock
Epic. "Last not merely first, but one
And only." It is too late to repair him.
He might as well be a window fallen
Into a flood upstate. He might as well
Tell once again the story of his beloved
Murdered, thrown to the trains as he
Watched the waters rising, glass himself.
Apocalypse is as you find it. North and south,
There is one last dream that will not be denied.

I am pretty well convinced that suicide
Explains the whales and the metal railings
At Battery Park. There is a consensus
Among drunkards that D.H. Lawrence's
Birds, Beasts and Flowers is a masterpiece:
"Where God is also love, but without words…".
The cathedral of Notre Dame burns as I write this.
The fire is the color of blood, a foxtail
Withering, architrave without a trace.
Without words, it is easier to trace
One million televised images back
To their source: the Actual Man mocking
The shattered glass of himself. Manhattan Island
Has only an ocean to offer and a drunkard's tremor.

Was the original flower a white one
Covering the island from end to end,
Not owned and not, therefore, in need of colors?
A white flower was the first window
Opened to the world. Human eyes
Could recognize themselves in the cluster,
Seeing the harmless sun shaped into petals,
Sensing a fathering and a mothering
In sunlight gentled there to simple vision.
Heaven is fine until the image of Heaven
Catches fire inside a cloud and comes to earth.
A welter of colors then, like animals in a panic,
Disturbs the sun out of its innocence,
And the white flowers are blind then.

With our own eyes, you and I have loved
One another in a crowd of images,

In a snare of garlands only now
Remembered as the lovely young people
Fifty years ago when Manhattan felt
Like a real island and not like a madhouse
Grievance bulwarked against flowers and faith.
Victimhood has robbed the sun of its innocence.
Mockery, which is a kind of murder,
Has stolen into the language and fingers
Of the city, producing a stammer
Of obscenities and a tremor
Of burnt matches at our fingers' ends.
I wish that all these words were raindrops.

"Out of the clouds," says Actual Man,
"A foxtail of rain covers the churches
And one by one the churches disappear."
Ave Verum Corpus is all well and good
For a gateway, but when the iron gates
Have rusted shut against the iron air
Choirs gasp, words die in the throat,
And the only sound is thorns underfoot,
A rustle as of bones shifting
Underground. Posterity is abandoned
To imaginary animals.
Race abdicates. Gender abdicates.
The color is disappearing from my hands
Like a vixen through a snare of garlands.

EPICUREAN

The misbelieving, as of a leaf caught fire out of frost,
Taunts the new day. It is the same tree, always the same,
And never time enough for actual blossom. A true white
Cabbage moth rises into it, as glad of frost as of fire.
It believes, and all the evidence is in its favor.
Green today or green eventually makes no difference.
Wings are wings, given to gladness as to weightlessness
In favor of flight. I was heavy and absent at the end.
The kill in cold or in desolating fever
Made an imbecile of me—nothing to choose between,
Nothing to distinguish but colors fading into luxury.
Every leaf is a model, every moth a cardiac event
Of empty air shown not to be empty, but killing
At blossom time, heavy with faith and scent.

CANANDAIGUA

My love / exists to prove you impossible.
— DONALD BRITTON

We love onto the exit,
A little rain and the town
Not unwilling: Kiwanis;
Quick service; actual geese
Going easy amidst children.

Easy, too, both to remember
And to find a shoe parlor,
The Merry-Go-Round,
And those same children
Standing over the X-ray,
Wiggling bones inside their toes.

The uncanny comes to us in odd
Numbers along the toll roads.
Rain is the reason, and old pains
Have emptied the public library so
That only the bare shelves show
One hour, one eighteenth birthday.
Benevolence was all the rage
For distant lakes, familiar ponds.
Today is a labor of windows

Whited with disuse and birdlime.
Get back into the car. Love me
Where never once you found me:
The next exit, the not unwilling town.

NOTES

"Spartoi"—the mythical soldiers who sprang up from dragon's teeth sown in the earth by Cadmus, King of Thebes.

"Communards"
1) Communards were the supporters and defenders of the doomed Paris Commune (March 18 through May 28, 1871). 10,000 to 15,000 Communards were executed; 7500 were jailed or deported.
2) Georges-Eugène Haussmann (1809-1891) was the urban planner hired by Napoleon III to renovate the city of Paris.
3) Robert Moses (1888-1981) was an urban developer in the metropolitan New York area. His designs favored highway systems over public transit.

"L'esiliato rientrava nel paese incorrotto"—a line from Eugenio Montale's poem "Mediterranean." William Arrowsmith translates the line as "The exile returned to his uncorrupted home."

"White-Jacket"—the title is that of a novel published in London by Herman Melville in 1850.

"Arrival at Emmaus"
1) For the story of Christ's post-resurrection appearance on the road to Emmaus, see the Gospel of Luke 24:13-35.

2) Baroque master Caravaggio painted his *The Supper at Emmaus* in 1601.

"Psaltery"—an ancient musical instrument consisting of a flat sounding box with numerous strings which are plucked with the fingers or with a plectrum.

ACKNOWLEDGMENTS

I wish to thank the editors of the following publications in which some of these poems first appeared:

The American Poetry Review
Beall Poetry Festival Broadsides
The Cincinnati Review
Clade Song
Conduit
Conjunctions
Glimpse
New American Writing
The Paris Review
Peripheries
Plume
Plume Poetry 8
Weber — The Contemporary West

RECENT TITLES FROM ALICE JAMES BOOKS

In the Days That Followed, Kevin Goodan
Light Me Down: The New & Collected Poems of Jean Valentine,
    Jean Valentine
Song of My Softening, Omotara James
Theophanies, Sarah Ghazal Ali
Orders of Service, Willie Lee Kinard III
The Dead Peasant's Handbook, Brian Turner
The Goodbye World Poem, Brian Turner
The Wild Delight of Wild Things, Brian Turner
I Am the Most Dangerous Thing, Candace Williams
Burning Like Her Own Planet, Vandana Khanna
Standing in the Forest of Being Alive, Katie Farris
Feast, Ina Cariño
Decade of the Brain: Poems, Janine Joseph
American Treasure, Jill McDonough
We Borrowed Gentleness, J. Estanislao Lopez
Brother Sleep, Aldo Amparán
Sugar Work, Katie Marya
Museum of Objects Burned by the Souls in Purgatory,
    Jeffrey Thomson
Constellation Route, Matthew Olzmann
How to Not Be Afraid of Everything, Jane Wong
Brocken Spectre, Jacques J. Rancourt
No Ruined Stone, Shara McCallum
The Vault, Andrés Cerpa
White Campion, Donald Revell
Last Days, Tamiko Beyer
If This Is the Age We End Discovery, Rosebud Ben-Oni
Pretty Tripwire, Alessandra Lynch
Inheritance, Taylor Johnson

Alice James Books is committed to publishing books that matter. The press was founded in 1973 in Boston, Massachusetts to give women access to publishing. As a cooperative, authors performed the day-to-day undertakings of the press. The press continues to expand and grow from its formative roots, guided by its founding values of access, excellence, inclusivity, and collaboration in publishing. Its mission is to publish books that matter and preserve a place of belonging for poets who inspire us. AJB seeks to broaden our collective interpretation of what constitutes the American poetic voice and is dedicated to helping its artists achieve purposeful engagement with broad audiences and communities nationwide. The press was named for Alice James, sister to William and Henry, whose extraordinary gift for writing went unrecognized during her lifetime.

Designed by Alban Fischer

Printed by Sheridan Saline